The Neglected Majority: Facilities for Commuting Students

Educational Facilities Laboratories

A report from EFL

REF
LB
2864
.E42
1977

Library of Congress Catalog No. 77-79050
First printing July 1977
©1977 by Educational Facilities Laboratories
Copies of this report are available for $4.00 prepaid
from EFL, 850 Third Avenue, New York, N.Y. 10022

Contents

Foreword, 5

What Nonresident Students Want on Campus, 6

Places To Study, 15

Places To Eat, 21

Places For Many Purposes, 27

Places To Park or Catch A Ride, 36

Places To Get Information, 41

Places To Leave Children, 46

Places To Rest, 48

Places For Recreation, 53

Places To Enjoy the Arts, 57

Places To Shop, 62

Other Services, 65

Managing the Change, 69

National Clearinghouse for Commuter Programs, 73

EFL **Publications, 74**

Foreword

There is no national organization making militant demands, but throughout the country students who do not live in college housing are asserting their rights to the same amenities for study, enrichment, and recreation that residential students receive. The vast majority of students live off campus, and administrators are beginning to realize that this constituency deserves better than it has been receiving.

Except for ivy-walled enclaves, a typical institution of higher education is attended by adults who work during the day, by students in their twenties who work full-time or part-time on a regular basis, who live at home or in shared apartments, and by adults who attend for enrichment, not for credits. Not surprisingly these people want places to study between classes, places to eat at irregular hours, and places to enjoy themselves or enrich themselves culturally. Too often the facilities provided for residential students are not convenient in location or scheduling for the commuting students.

The Neglected Majority: Facilities for Commuting Students reports on activities and facilities related to providing services for nonresidents at several colleges and universities. They range from new student unions to minor services that cost practically nothing to provide.

Two members of EFL's staff worked on this publication: Larry Molloy directed the project and Vicki Moses undertook the research. The manuscript is by Velma Adams, an education writer.

The Neglected Majority is part of a project on higher education facilities supported by The Andrew W. Mellon Foundation. Two other titles are being published with this report, *Space Costing: Who Should Pay For the Use of College Space?* and *Housing For New Types of Students*. The foundation also supported two earlier reports, *Generating Revenue from College Facilities* and *Campus in Transition*.

EDUCATIONAL FACILITIES LABORATORIES

What Nonresident Students Want on Campus

Commuting students enrolled in the nation's colleges and universities outnumber their residential counterparts by about three to one. They form a diverse group that includes day and evening students, "regular" students and continuing education students, young persons and mature adults, full-time and part-time students. Within their ranks are numerous subgroups with special needs: graduate students, employed students, handicapped students, married students, parents, and veterans, as examples.

The only characteristic that uniquely distinguishes commuting students as a group is that its members do not live on campus. They pay the same—or higher—tuition per credit hour that resident students pay. (Many states do not regulate the fees charged by public colleges for extension and continuing education courses.) Often they are assessed fees for student services they do not use and for activities in which they have little time to participate. But their number is increasing—even on nonurban campuses.

Until recently, the traditional colleges and universities have paid little attention to the needs of this new majority. The reason seems to be less a matter of money than a reluctance on the part of administrators and institutions to make a commitment to change. They have been slow to ask what commuting students want or to observe their behavior and traffic patterns. Yet the studies and surveys that have been done reveal that the expectations of such students are modest and conventional. Often they can be satisfied without a great capital investment, by reallocating existing resources, renovating space and making cosmetic changes, and rescheduling some activities.

Essentially what commuting students lack is a base from which to operate, a place to hang their hats. They need facilities to park their cars and their bicycles, to place their belongings and their children, to study, to grab a quick bite, or take a short nap; they need "hangouts" where they can meet friends or play a casual game of ping pong or pool—in short, places in which they feel they belong and can spend their time on campus productively.

Often the solutions—converting existing spaces to different uses; adding a little paint, some equipment, and furnishings; changing the schedule; and decentralizing and diversifying services, such as food services, to make them available at more places and hours—require more imagination than dollars. Yet the response on most campuses has been slow. The reasons for the establishment's neglect of the new majority are several:

☐ The traditional image of a college student as an 18-to-24-year-old who lives on campus for four or more years still prevails. There are "deans who still tend to make part-time study appear a social disgrace and an academic weakness," writes Fred M. Hechinger in *Saturday Review* (September 20, 1975). "Colleges should overcome their own static view of themselves as enclaves reserved largely for post-adolescent resident students...."

☐ College administrators, many of whom were educated at colleges with residency requirements, have not adjusted themselves to the commuters who swarm over campus at peak hours, often in the late afternoon and evening after many of the regular faculty and staff have gone home, and who leave campus for home or job as soon as the classes they are attending are over. Although it is an old-fashioned view, many administrations still look down on "subway circuit" students and treat them as second-class citizens in the college community. They are separate and not equal.

☐ Residential students are a more homogeneous group, perceived by administrators as easier to deal with than the diverse commuters, whose reasons for enrolling may be as varied as their backgrounds. They may be older than their instructors and more experienced, seeking additional knowledge and skills to help them move up the organizational ladder or to avoid becoming obsolete. They may be preparing to change careers or to enter the job market for the first time. Or they may be no older than the residential students, simply young people from low-income families and perhaps the first generation to go to college even part-time. Together these two

groups constitute this decade's boom in higher education.
☐ Commuting students, until recently, have had no advocate. In the early 1970s, several colleges with growing commuter populations, such as the University of Maryland, Kutztown (Pa.) State College, and Oakland University (Rochester, Mich.), established an Office for Commuter Affairs. A director and a small staff, generally commuting students working part-time, set about educating administrators, raising the awareness of the campus community to its current clientele, and pushing for funding and approval for some of the facilities and services that commuting students need most.

Commuters and their concerns

The number of nonresident students in the country can be measured, but no one has the resources to ascertain what kinds of people live off campus and walk or travel to school each day. One or two colleges have surveyed their commuting students and drawn a profile, but it seems rash to extrapolate such findings on a national scale.

Some observers assert that commuters are apt to be older, employed, more serious about their studies and more pragmatic about the relationship of the curriculum to their careers than residential students. They carry heavier financial and family responsibilities, and maintain closer ties with their families and friends—and with the culture and mores—in the neighborhoods in which they grew up. Many are married and have families of their own; some are heads of single-parent households. Demands on their time, the tight schedules they follow, influence everything they do—the courses they enroll in, the activities they pursue, the time they spend on campus, where and how they spend it.

The educational effect of the time constraints is serious. Commuting students must balance their pursuit of knowledge with the exigencies of class schedules. Thus, many commuters are reported to select courses and majors more on the basis of when and where classes meet than on content. They try to avoid free periods between classes and returning to campus a second time in one day. Wayne State University found that commuting students were staying away from field trips and on-campus events because it is too difficult to rearrange their schedules and to stretch their budgets to include an extra meal or carfare.

The commuter profile, already a far cry from that of the adult who takes a noncredit hobby or enrichment course, is changing yearly. A study of freshmen commuting students at the University of Maryland for the years 1973 through 1975 showed that in the latter years more commuters had fathers with college degrees and more intended to study beyond the bachelor degree level.

The largest percentage of commuting students at the university is in the age range from 25 to 34 years old, but 40-, 50-, and 60-year-olds are by no means uncommon. In a 1973 survey, more than 60 percent of the 26,000 commuters were employed, and 28 percent of these reported that they worked more than 20 hours a week. Many were employed full-time. Considering the number of employed and the increasing number of women with children who are returning to college, it is not hard to see why time, and aids to its efficient use, are major concerns of college commuters.

Except for the fortunate few who live on the fringes of campus, commuting students spend from half an hour to more than an hour getting from home to campus. They may work at a third location. Their total weekly commuting time, plus the frustrating minutes during which they look for parking spaces or wait for buses or subways, may amount to more time than they spend on campus. Many of them certainly consume more time traveling and working at their jobs than resident students spend attending class and studying.

More than 60 percent of the commuting students at the University of Maryland report no participation in extracurricular activities, even as spectators. Attending an evening speaker series may require four or five extra hours on campus, loss of pay, less study time, and an extra meal to buy.

Commuting students everywhere cite "low cost" as the major reason for their nonresidential status. "Near home" and "convenient to work" are also significant factors, helping to keep the cost down and making attendance at college possible.

"Opportunities for growth experiences are lost in the gap

between home and school," point out Mark W. Hardwick and Martha P. Kazlo in their study, "A Model for Change," which led to the establishment of an Office of Commuter Student Affairs at the University of Maryland. Hardwick and Kazlo found that the personal independence of commuters is limited. Many are first generation college attenders who are seeking to change their social and economic status, but whose parents expect them to act the same and adhere to the same values as previously. Consequently, the commuting student is less likely than his counterpart who lives on campus to be free to examine and experiment with new social and political ideas.

A large percentage of a commuter's friendships are "left over" from high school. Building meaningful relationships with faculty and staff—and even with other students—is a problem. The commuter's life is termed "the divided life" by Richard F. Ward and Theodore E. Kurz in *The Commuting Student: A Study of Facilities at Wayne State University*. Evidence of the split can be seen on campus in the schedule, the environment, and the facilities.

What commuters crave

One economical and functional response to the unmet needs of commuter students—and the structure on which they have had the biggest impact to date—is a centrally located student center or union that is designed or renovated as a multiuse facility offering many services under one roof. Excellent examples of student unions that have been enlarged and renovated with the commuting students in mind can be found at the University of Minnesota, the University of Oregon, and at North Texas State University.

Specifically what commuting students say they need most are the following: study areas; meeting and eating places; lounge space; places to sleep (especially at exam time); parking spaces; transportation between buildings and to public transit lines; lockers; recreational areas with equipment; child care centers; and information and message centers.

"Conveniently located" is the commuters' slogan. Facilities on class-to-class or class-to-car paths get the most use. The appeal of lounges where resident and nonresident can stop to talk, study, or relax together is enhanced if there are fast food services nearby.

"Commuters have less time for activities than residents," says Stephen Tibbitts, Director of Non-Residence Life at Kutztown State College, "but many of their problems are the same. They need many of the same services and some different ones, but there is no place where they can get them unless a campus has an office for commuter students."

Kutztown established its office in 1972 in recognition that nearly 50 percent of the student body was commuting. Now 2,100 of the 4,000 undergraduates live at home or in town.

"We are still experimenting with facilities and scheduling suited to their needs," says Tibbitts. "It is taking time for colleges to wake up and acknowledge the trend."

Why respond?

There are convincing reasons for responding positively to commuter students. Their growing number, of course, heads the list. They have become higher education's major clientele, its "typical" students. For some institutions, wooing them successfully may mean survival.

Mark W. Hardwick and Martha P. Kazlo, authors of the prospectus for the University of Maryland's commuter services program, estimated that in 1974, 75 percent of all college students were commuting; they expect a 90 percent commuting rate by 1985.

At the same time, a significant drop in full-time residential students is projected. The pool of 18-to-21-year-olds will peak within the next five years, then shrink from 17 to 13.5 million within ten years. How many of them will elect to go to college as residents immediately after high school is unpredictable. The continuation rate has been dropping steadily for several years and does not appear to have bottomed out yet.

The demand for higher education among individuals over 21, however, is still growing. A rapidly changing labor market is sending many adults back to college to add to their knowledge and skills in order to move up in their professions, to change fields, or simply to avoid becoming obsolete. Those who took early retirement are seeking new interests. Women and minorities, encouraged by affirmative action, are seeking training for new careers. Competition to get them to enroll is bound to increase.

Large numbers of adults, phasing in and out of higher education, may help to lift its value and restore public confidence. Commuters are proving to be both good students and valuable alumni, forming a useful link between college and community. Graduates of Hood College in Frederick, Maryland, recently helped to raise funds for county scholarships. Alumni of several institutions have been instrumental in getting "town and gown" cooperation on public transportation and on traffic and parking problems. Obviously, avoiding students with no ties or loyalty to their alma mater can pay off.

On campus, the influence of commuter students is growing. While only a handful of colleges have offices for commuter students, more than 100 institutions have identified personnel in their offices of student affairs, continuing education, and in other offices who have job responsibilities or interests directly related to commuter students. The National Clearinghouse for Commuter Programs, with headquarters at the University of Maryland, provides an information exchange. The staff of the University's Office of Commuter Services doubles as the staff of the Clearinghouse. The newsletter, *The Commuter*, formerly a quarterly, will be published monthly this year at the University of South Florida in Tampa. Also operating on a national, as well as a regional, scale to plan for the commuter phenomenon is the Commuter Task Force of the American College Personnel Association's Commission II.

Plans for accommodating commuter students naturally will vary according to the circumstances on each campus and on the local student input. There are many changes that can make life easier and more productive for commuting students. One of the objectives of an office for commuter services is to convince college administrations and state legislatures to change policies and to allocate funds, even in small amounts, to carry out some of the ideas already on the drawing boards.

How can you adapt your buildings to better serve the human needs of users? Some examples of what other colleges and universities are doing may help you to decide.

Oversize landings with tables and chairs provide spaces for study and conversation at California State University.

Places To Study

Commuting students, when questioned about their needs, almost unanimously assign top priority to more study areas. Surveys report students using stairways, window sills, and parked cars as locations in which to read and write. They have no dorm rooms and few quiet places to study at home. They want more such spaces on campus, conveniently located, easily accessible, informal, where they can drop in, maybe smoke and snack while they catch up on their homework. Mentioned also as desirable aids are reference rooms, study carrels, department lounges, and typing rooms. Hood College's library, for example, has separate study hours for day students and extra audiovisual equipment particularly for the use of graduate students after 4 P.M.

In 1971, before beginning construction of the Auraria Higher Education Center in Denver, three Colorado institutions—the University of Colorado Denver Center, Metropolitan State College, and the Community College of Denver-Auraria—surveyed more than 16,000 students. Forty-three percent rated their home study conditions fair to very poor, but less than a quarter of the total sample was satisfied with the study facilities on their campuses. They described them as "too crowded," "too noisy," "inconveniently located," and in some instances, "badly lighted." Students indicated that they studied in public libraries, at work, while traveling, at a friend's or relative's home, or in areas at school not specifically designated for study, such as empty classrooms, restaurants, and school eating facilities. Conclusion: study areas should be widely dispersed throughout the campus to encourage their use between classes as well as for longer periods. In response, Denver's Auraria Higher Education Center, to be completed in January 1977 for an anticipated 20,000 students, has ten study lounges in as many locations around the campus. There is also a central media center with closed circuit television capability. Write: *Fredye Wright, Public Information Director, P.O. Box 4615, Denver, Colo. 80204.*

Places to study

Nooks and crannies in the building can be put to use as informal studying spaces (1). Custom-designed seating captures space for studying without giving an institutional look (2). Comfortable but easily moved chairs combined with reading lamps create attractive corner for reading or gazing (3). Study spaces should also provide for students who do not require silence. Guitarist plays in background of former barbershop (4). All pictures taken at the University of Oregon.

3

4

Places to study

The University of Maryland operates a study lodge for commuters during exam week. Located in the Cambridge Community Center, the lodge is open 24 hours a day. In addition to a place to study and a xerox machine, the lodge offers a place to sleep, including a bed, bedding, and a wake-up service; a snack bar and free coffee from 1 A.M. on; and a place to relax with TV, games, and magazines. A staff member, who is available to answer questions, also maintains a locked room for storing students' belongings. Reservations must be made, but students need only dial Call-a-Ride and a shuttle bus will pick up and deliver them to the lodge. Write: *Sylvia Stewart, Director, Office of Commuter Affairs, University of Maryland, 1211 Student Union, College Park, Md. 20742.*

When students at California State College in Los Angeles were asked to develop their own requirements for a new student union they included provision for private, semiprivate, and public study spaces. Some are on wide balconies around a four-story atrium topped with a skylight. Oversized stair landings with tables and chairs facilitate study or talk and double as performing stages and spectator galleries for cultural events. In one section, spherical chairs with loudspeakers are built into the sides at ear level. Ash trays in certain areas indicate where smoking is permitted. Scattered throughout the building are numerous drop-in study rooms with doors that close to ensure quiet, and plenty of spaces for a ten-minute eat-smoke-and-study session. The borrowing library also permits both smoking and eating. Write: *Director of Student Union, California State College, 5151 State University Drive, Los Angeles, Calif. 90032.*

Students also influenced the facilities at the Erb Memorial Union at the University of Oregon. The overcrowded building of 1950 vintage has been supplemented with an addition of 60,000 sq ft, and underused and out-of-date areas have been adapted for new uses. Custom-made tables and chairs arranged in an undulating snakelike formation down a long, wide corridor provide space for studying or lounging without interfering with the pedestrian traffic. A living-studying room, carpeted and with traditional furniture and a fireplace, offers a quieter atmosphere. Window sills around the building have been turned into study nooks by installing upholstered seats and backrests. And for students who want even more informality, the barber chairs and waiting benches were left in the former barbershop. Write: *Adele McMillan, Director, Erb Memorial Union, University of Oregon, Eugene, Ore. 97403.*

There are about 2,000 spaces for study in various buildings throughout the University of Minnesota's Twin Cities campus. Some are restricted to students in the various colleges, but the study area of the main campus library, Wilson Memorial Library on the West Bank, is open from 7 A.M. to 1 A.M., Monday through Thursday. It closes at 10 P.M. on Friday and the Saturday hours are from 9 A.M. to 6 P.M. Sunday hours are from noon to 1 A.M. The study area is open 24 hours during final week.

The Coffman Union was remodeled in 1976. Low partitions divide the lounge areas on the first floor to create small meeting and studying areas. A commuter lounge area located near the entrance to a new theater-lecture hall has a carpeted section for students who prefer to sit on the floor.

Students who belong to a fraternity or sorority have another choice. The Greeks have a special arrangement for members who commute that includes not only a place to study but also parking at little or no cost. They may have some meals at the house and if necessary, at final exam time, sleep overnight. Write: *Ronaele Sayre, Information Representative, Department of University Relations, S-68 Morrill Hall, Minneapolis, Minn. 55455.*

The University of South Florida makes a distinction between its academic study lounges and its leisure lounge locations. There are about 25 study rooms in the various colleges and departments and 165 study rooms available in the library. There is a room designated as a leisure lounge in five of the nine colleges, as well as in the science center, the faculty office building, and the library. Write: *Charles F. Hewitt, Student Affairs, ADM 151, University of South Florida, Tampa, Fla. 33620.*

Student Union, University of California at Berkeley

Places To Eat

Perhaps the biggest mistake traditional residential colleges make in dealing with commuter students is to consider food facilities as merely a way to provide food and drink. Eating places are also important for socializing with other students; for meeting with faculty; for study, especially group study; for recreation; for relaxing; for waiting for the next class; and even for napping. Eating times bear little relationship to conventional dining hours. A study done prior to the building of the Auraria Higher Education Center in Denver showed that the peak use of eating facilities correlates with class schedules, not with meal times. A variety of places to stop, talk, read, or compare notes while getting a quick bite is imperative if students are to stay on campus for any length of time. All sorts of fast food services—snack bars, cafeterias, coffeehouses, specialty spots serving ethnic and health foods, vending machines, and "brown bag" lunch areas—are popular, especially if they are small and near a lounge, in a multipurpose building, or on class-to-class or class-to-car paths where traffic is heavy.

This trend away from dining rooms serving full meals at specified hours was not generated exclusively by commuting students although they are certainly a major factor in the change. Residential students also often balk at the lack of flexibility in hours and menus by boycotting dormitory dining rooms even when it means sacrificing the price of their meal tickets. Like their commuting peers, they want the freedom to satisfy their own tastes and timetables. The more casual meeting and eating places encourage conversation and social interaction that can benefit both resident and commuter, whereas separate dining rooms are a divisive influence.

A study sponsored by the Research and Information Committee of ACUHO (Association of College and University Housing Officers) reveals that only a small percentage of colleges and universities offer food services and residence hall programs specifically designed to meet commuting students' needs. Roughly one half of the institutions surveyed make food service facilities available to commuters, but only 24 percent offer food plans such as lunch only or some other flexible arrangement to serve commuters. Johns Hopkins University considers it important enough for commuters to eat some meals in the dormitory cafeteria with their fellow freshmen that the college issues discount meal tickets to commuters.

At a number of institutions, students take an active part in providing adequate food services. There is a student cooperative dining facility in the University of Maryland student union, for example, and student associations at UCLA and elsewhere manage the food services in the student center.

Going along with the trend to diversified food services can save, and sometimes make, money for the colleges. Franchised food services have proved successful on many campuses where traditional facilities were losing money. Usually the franchisee renovates, decorates, and equips the facility and pays the institution a percentage of the gross sales.

Admittedly, negotiating contracts with fast food chains and food vending companies, monitoring their performance, and making changes from time to time to suit the demand may bring a whole new set of problems for administrators. But if colleges do not capitalize on the students' preference for eating informally and at unscheduled hours as a way to generate some income for the institution, commercial interests in the vicinity of the campus will. Where new approaches have been tried—and examples are numerous—results have been favorable.

Franchised food services are proving profitable for the University of Cincinnati, where McDonald's opened its first campus restaurant in 1973 in the Tangeman University Center. Since then a number of other food vendors have moved into the center. Previously, the university's food services operation, run by a single contractor, was facing a deficit of $150,000, and the university decided it had to take a look at other systems.

The Tangeman Center, built in 1937 and enlarged to double its original size in 1965, housed a huge kitchen supplying five different dining areas. Large staffs, high wages, little variety in the menus, and students staying away in droves convinced the university to take a critical look at its food services. The outcome was that the university replaced its single contract food service with agreements with a number of individual restaurants.

Fast food franchise at Ohio State University

McDonald's, first to be granted a lease, moved into the remodeled and redecorated cafeteria. Prices are the same as off campus and there is no waiting for service. Mr. Jim's Steakhouse, LaRose's Pizza, and Boerger's New Orleans Ice Cream Shop followed; these offer a variety of eating options to the 28,000 students, 75 percent of whom are commuters. A Chicago catering firm operates a formal dining room for those who desire such facilities. Food sales at Tangeman increased from $557,000 in 1972-73 to $1,109,549 in 1973-74, a 100 percent increase. Colleges whose food services are not paying their way may benefit from giving serious consideration to leasing and franchising. Write: *Richard J. Towner, Director, Tangeman University Center, University of Cincinnati, Cincinnati, Ohio 45221.*

Finding cost-effective ways to feed massive constituencies on large campuses is a challenge. Ohio State University, with more than 50,000 students, has completely revised its all-or-nothing meal plan policy and welcomed franchised and vending machine food services. At cafeterias in five locations, students have a choice of eating one meal a day or up to 20 meals a week. Tickets are less expensive if purchased in multiples of ten and are good at all five locations. This year's participation by 900 nonresidents is a 17 percent increase over last year.

The west campus, where 2,800 to 3,000 freshmen per hour have classes, previously had only vending machines. Full-blown food service, it was decided, could not be run profitably by the university. Instead, the university asked for bids from commercial food vendors. Burger King, which got the contract, paid for the site renovation. The university gets a percentage of the restaurant's gross income. About 550 students a day transfer their noon meal ticket from their residence halls to the Burger King on the west campus. This has enabled the university to reduce its bus service between the main and west campus, thus lowering fuel and maintenance costs. Write: *Dr. John Nelson, Assistant V.P., Ohio State University, 1800 Cannon Drive, Columbus, Ohio 43220.*

A lot of learning in college takes place outside the classroom. Commuters get very little opportunity to experience this unless the institutions provide the opportunity. Hood College runs a series of "learning lunches" to pull together campus and community. Townspeople as well as day and residential students are invited to the lounge of the continuing education center for a brown-bag luncheon with a program. Programs include book reviews, films, music, and speakers. Featured recently was the wife of a senatorial candidate describing what life is like for a candidate's wife. There have been other lectures on a wide variety of topics including death and dying, abortion, and "save the whales." A jazz program pulled well. Average attendance last year was 42, but as many as 69 have crowded into the lounge at once with the extras sitting on the carpeted floor. Sponsors report a good mix of day and residential students and community members, who otherwise would have to go to Washington, D.C., or Baltimore for this type of program. Hood College also has a brown-bag area with kitchen facilities in its Rayford Lodge, an old house renovated as a home-away-from-home for day students. Write: *Dixie Miller, Director, Department of Continuing Education, Hood College, Frederick, Md. 21701.*

With few choices in restaurant facilities on campus, students at C.W. Post College, a branch of Long Island University, N.Y., were going off campus for coffee and food. Hillwood Commons, the new student union, has cut down the daily exodus. Now students may choose among a variety of facilities and food offerings all under one roof. The Commons—next door to "The Dome," a 3,000-seat theater and auditorium whose programs attract the public as well as the college community—includes a snack bar, a cafeteria, the Rathskeller, offering folksinging along with the beer, wine, and delicatessen sandwiches, and the Top-of-the-Commons restaurant and cocktail lounge for both faculty and students. The Rathskeller is open until midnight Monday through Thursday and until 1 A.M. on Friday and Saturday. Write: *Joseph H. Benedict, Jr., Director, Hillwood Commons, C.W. Post College, Greenvale, N.Y. 11548.*

At the University of California's Los Angeles campus, the Associated Students of UCLA, an independent student association, plays an aggressive role in providing a wide range of food services. They see this as part of their association's basic goal to enhance the quality of life for the 33,000 students and for the entire campus community. Annual sales from food facilities and vending machines total $3.3 million.

Student Union at UCLA

Places to eat

Because of the campus size, the students felt they needed eating facilities at numerous locations within easy walking distance of classes. Among the interesting options are a restaurant called The World's Wurst Sausages, and the Treehouse Cafeteria with four serving lanes: one leading to a make-it-yourself salad bar and sandwich area, one for natural foods and vegetarian items, and two lanes for standard menus. The Kerckhoff Coffee House serves ice cream and crepes, and adds entertainment in the evening. The Bombshelter and Deli Bar, as its name implies, is a fast-food delicatessen. The Coop features hamburgers and hot dogs, and the Campus Corner offers authentic Mexican food. Most food is sold between 11 A.M. and 2 P.M., but food centers stagger their hours to meet the needs of students until 11 P.M. At most locations, there is outdoor as well as indoor seating, and vending machines are scattered throughout the campus. Write: *Don Finley, Director, Associated Students of UCLA, Kerckhoff Hall, 405 Hilgard Avenue, Los Angeles, Calif. 90024.*

One of the most economical ways for colleges to give commuter students more options in food service hours, menus, and prices is to install food vending machines. They may require some changes in staffing patterns and facilities, but generally only minor building renovations are involved. They can be fitted into odd-shaped and little-used areas in classroom buildings, libraries and lounges, or along corridors where traffic is heavy. If traffic patterns or other conditions change, reducing the demand, vending machines can be moved easily and inexpensively. Capital outlay is small and little servicing is required by college personnel. Consequently, this is a type of food service on which offices of commuter services can have an immediate impact. The Office of Commuter Services at Oakland University, by means of a survey, identified a number of problem areas on campus. Personnel are now working with the business office on specifications and contracts with vendors to improve service. The changes involve some space modification near the lounges. Write: *Rosalind Andreas, Director of Commuter Services, Oakland University, Rochester, Mich. 48063.*

Places For Many Purposes

As commuter student populations increase, many colleges are finding their student centers or unions inadequate in size and too limited in the scope of services provided. Often the most satisfactory and economical solution is a multiuse facility serving a whole range of physical, social and psychological needs. Ideally, such a multipurpose student center, whether new or renovated, is centrally located; the campus that has such space or a building suitable for conversion near the center of the campus is fortunate. The former concept of a lounge as a separate entity—a place to while away time idly apart from other activities—is fast becoming archaic. Students, particularly commuting students, want the convenience and casualness of combining or alternating their activities—eating while they study, interspersing study with conversation and recreation, arranging rides or doing other necessary errands without having to trek across campus or downtown. The closer to heavily used walkways the better. Student centers that house lounges, study rooms or carrels, small meeting rooms, offices for student affairs and student associations, eating facilities, some modest recreational facilities, lockers, and an information or message center—or provide at least several of these services—are the most useful and efficient for both students and the institution.

North Texas State University more than doubled the size of its student union by remodeling an existing 90,000 square feet and enclosing it in an additional 120,000 square feet. The result is a combination of indoor and outdoor spaces that sprawl down a hillside connecting a library mall with a two-block long mall leading to the Art Building precisely in the center of the campus. Because of the sloping site, The Union may be entered from the ground at three levels.

The building functions as a self-contained city with its own post office, a newsstand, a store, a 500-seat theater equipped for movies as well as live stage productions, a ticket reservation booth, and a variety of places for meeting, eating, studying, and relaxing. The Union serves 16,000 students, 80 percent of whom are commuters. More than half of the commuters live outside Denton. Their home away from home is the Commuter Room on the lower level of The Union. Coin lockers are available for storing extra gear, and a special lounge for women students serves as a retreat where they can relax between classes. Other distinctive features of The Union, some practical and some purely for pleasure, include the following:

☐ The Gallery, which features traveling art shows as well as special university exhibits.

☐ An arts and crafts room on the lower level where instructors help with ceramics, metal-working, jewelry-making, and other crafts.

☐ The Avesta Room, a quiet retreat where students can listen to music, read, or relax, with a roaring blaze in the fireplace in the winter.

☐ A television viewing room with a four-foot screen.

☐ The O'Clock Lounge. Just down the hall from the Avesta and TV rooms, this is a large, open lounge with terraced, carpeted seating where people can meet informally.

☐ The Rock Bottom Lounge, with the atmosphere of a small club, serves up deli sandwiches and live music nightly.

☐ The Campus Chat is The Union's snack bar. It has a working fireplace.

☐ The Balcony, adjacent to the Campus Chat and overlooking the courtyard, offers more formal dining. From the courtyard in the center of the lower level one can look upward from a cascading brook, past a giant tree and three floors of facilities to the skylight at the top.

Offices and meeting rooms abound, accommodating from 8 to 800 persons at one time. On the third floor there are two forum rooms with tiered seating, raised platforms, and motorized projection screens (capacity: 76 and 44); six meeting rooms, three seating 48 and one each seating 8, 16, and 30; and a seminar room seating 8. Student organizations have their offices on this floor, while the university's offices of student services, financial aid, placement, and counseling are clustered together on the second floor for the convenience of students. Covered walkways outdoors provide student organizations a place to set up registration tables and hold sales and exhibits.

Because of The Union's ample dimensions, North Texas State has not had to sacrifice its large banquet and meeting rooms to make space for more casual eating and meeting places. Both the smaller banquet room on the second floor (capacity: 140) and the Silver Eagle Room on the top floor (capacity: 800) can be partitioned into three areas seating smaller groups. Write: *Dorothy Pijan, Director of The Union, North Texas State University, Denton, Tex. 76203.*

Responses to commuter needs can be modest and at the same time effective. As part of its effort to encourage commuting students, Hood College has done over an old house for the use of day students. Known as Rayford Lodge, the renovated house contains kitchen facilities, including a refrigerator, a desk area with shared desk spaces for 100 or more students, and a quiet area with bunks for napping. Students can take brown-bag lunches and prepare their own food, eating what they prefer and keeping the cost down. The lodge provides a place to go between classes, to study, to meet others, and to wait for one's car pool. The Department of Continuing Education also serves as a meeting place, with a lounge, coffee machine, and typewriter available. In the last three years Hood's commuter population has jumped to 250 undergraduates, about 22 percent of the total number. All of the 450 graduate students are commuters. Write: *Dixie Miller, Director, Department of Continuing Education, Hood College, Frederick, Md. 21701.*

The University of Minnesota is just completing a $7 million renovation to its student center, built in 1938 for approximately $2 million. Plans for the remodeling of Coffman Union on the Minneapolis campus were based on a study of the traffic patterns both outside and within the building. The union, located near the dorms, serves both resident and commuter students, bringing them together for a wide range of activities. An estimated 75 percent of the total student body use the center. The remodeling, begun two years ago, is being carried out in stages, beginning with the basement and ground floors and working upward. The basement is given over to recreation and food service. Called the Gopher Hole, it houses bowling alleys, a swimming pool, pinball machines, a coffee house and cafeteria, and vending machines for quick access to soup, salad, sandwiches, and ice cream. An unusual feature is the microwave ovens where students heat their own food. The ground floor, reflecting the traffic patterns, is an attempt to convert wasted space into usable areas. A seldom-used entrance was closed, another one opened, and a glass wall installed facing the mall. Lounge areas have been expanded and mini-walls installed to make meeting spaces for small groups. There is a theater and lecture hall, with multimedia facilities and listening areas where students can listen to their own or borrowed tapes. Offices for all student organizations, formerly scattered about the campus, are now located in the second floor of Coffman. An intercampus bus serves the Minneapolis, St. Paul, and West Bank campuses. Write: *Ronaele Sayre, Information Representative, S-68 Morrill Hall, Minneapolis, Minn. 55455.*

A 1974 addition of 60,000 square feet to the University of Oregon's Erb Memorial Union and the accompanying reallocation of already existing space turned the building into a shopping center of student services. The new floor plan eliminates most of the traffic congestion and ensures that students en route to high-use areas, like food services, will be exposed to activities that they might otherwise ignore. The size, location, layout, and design of the remodeled union are the direct result of student input to the planning. Five students appointed by the student senate were voting members of the university campus planning committee and on a number of issues they were convincing enough to prevail. They were unanimous, for example, in their support for an addition to the existing union instead of a satellite union at another site which, they argued, would divide the student body and break down communications. They wanted a functional, down-to-earth usable building, not a showplace of bronze and marble. They saw no need for ballroom expansion nor for as much office and meeting room space as planners suggested; they preferred to increase and diversify food services and to include an arts and crafts center and a day care facility, neither of which would have been considered seriously when the union was built in 1950.

The emphasis is on circulation and distribution of traffic. There are entrances to the building on more than one level, so that pass-through traffic does not congest corridors, and ramps leading to the most-used service areas. The addition to Erb is organized around an open core with general public activities near the core and specific private activities along the periphery. On all three levels there are dining areas connected by ramps; outdoor terraces; and lounge/study spaces that provide a "living room" atmosphere and encourage personal contact among students, faculty, and staff.

The Erb Memorial Union contains a number of other features that are responsive to the emerging needs and life-styles of today's students:

☐ Six small meeting rooms and a large multipurpose meeting room that can be divided to accommodate two or more events

Meeting rooms double as classrooms at the University of Oregon

simultaneously. Unlike the meeting rooms in the original union, which were kept locked when not in scheduled use, the rooms in the addition can be used for studying, dining, and TV viewing when not reserved.

Erb Memorial Union, University of Oregon

☐ A crafts center, professionally staffed, provides space for ceramics, jewelry, leatherworking, woodworking, and photography. Instruction and materials are available on the site.
☐ Office spaces on the lower level of the addition are close to a central pedestrian passage, making them easily accessible.

They were designed for flexibility to accommodate the changing needs of student organizations from year to year. The campus newspaper took over the third floor office space in the original building.

☐ The Recreation Center on the ground level of Erb Memorial Union under the main lobby is open seven days a week for informal games. The bowling alley has 16 lanes, and shoes and bowling balls are available for rent. Bowling classes are conducted for academic credit. There are 16 billiard tables, 2 table tennis tables, and a regulation-size shuffleboard. Winners of campus tournaments in bowling, billiards, bridge, chess, and table tennis go on to regional and international competition.

☐ A print shop in the basement off a central passage includes the following among its expanded services: offset printing, enlargement and reduction, printing of theses and dissertations, stapling and collating, and sign and poster production.

☐ A child-care facility for use on a short-term drop-in basis aids students who want to attend a class or an event but do not require full-time day-care services. Write: *Adele McMillan, Director, Erb Memorial Union, University of Oregon, Eugene, Ore. 97403.*

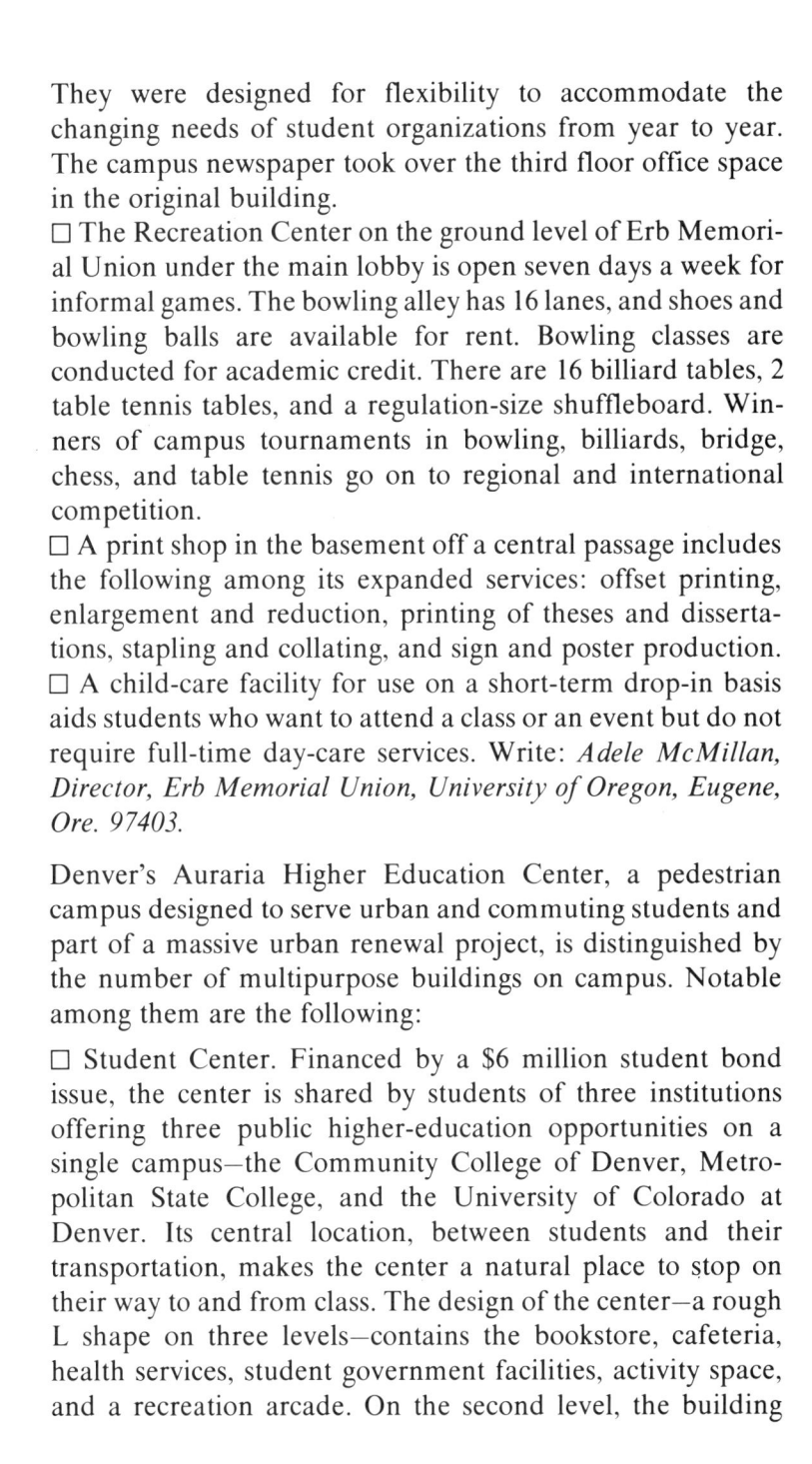

Denver's Auraria Higher Education Center, a pedestrian campus designed to serve urban and commuting students and part of a massive urban renewal project, is distinguished by the number of multipurpose buildings on campus. Notable among them are the following:

☐ Student Center. Financed by a $6 million student bond issue, the center is shared by students of three institutions offering three public higher-education opportunities on a single campus—the Community College of Denver, Metropolitan State College, and the University of Colorado at Denver. Its central location, between students and their transportation, makes the center a natural place to stop on their way to and from class. The design of the center—a rough L shape on three levels—contains the bookstore, cafeteria, health services, student government facilities, activity space, and a recreation arcade. On the second level, the building

Places for many purposes

Erb Memorial Union, University of Oregon

encloses a raised plaza or outdoor student forum. The cafeteria has immediate access to this space, allowing for outdoor eating. A terrace on the next higher level serves as a platform for the forum. A second-floor pedestrian bridge links this terrace to the Arts Building and the Physical Education Building.

☐ Tivoli Brewery. The redevelopment of the Tivoli Brewery and the connecting Turnhalle Opera House, to be completed in three years, will recreate the historic atmosphere of one of Colorado's pioneer businesses. Much of the original brewing equipment remains in the white structure with its blue mansard roof and 114-foot tower. Inside 135,480 usable square feet will be campus restaurants, stores, and entertainment facilities. Plans include a glass atrium surrounded by an ice-cream shop, a gallery, and an artisan workshop. There will be quick food service, a bakery, a bank, miscellaneous shops, and restaurants on various levels of the complex with a German beer garden opening onto a plaza and bazaar area. Three movie theaters are being built for use during the mornings by students and presenting feature entertainments in the afternoons and evenings. The Turnhalle Opera House will be restored for concerts and live theater productions. The work on Tivoli, which is located within easy walking distance of classes, is being done by a private developer.

☐ Ninth Street Historic Park. This is the oldest block of houses in Denver. Five of the 14 modest Victorian homes were built before Colorado became a state. The landmark structures are being renovated by private developers for use as faculty offices and for education-related programs. A grant from the National Endowment for the Arts has made possible creative landscaping of this adjunct to the Auraria campus.

The Auraria Higher Education Center, a $73-million complex, is an excellent example of what can be accomplished through collaboration. Buildings are being financed by the federal government, the state of Colorado, the city of Denver, private developers and—in the case of the student center and the child care center—by students. Write: *Floyd K. Stearns, Executive Director, Auraria Higher Education Center, 1068 - 9th Street, Denver, Colo. 80204.*

Places To Park or Catch A Ride

The first response of many institutions to the commuter influx was to build bigger parking lots. They were needed certainly, but in viep of the scarcity of space near many campuses and the other needs that commuting students have, more paved parking lots may not be the best investment of institutional funds. Other alternatives being used successfully are partially subsidized public transportation; shuttle buses from key points on the public transportation system or from parking areas away from the campus; more public parking near the campus; incentives to car pooling; safe bicycle parking;

Mt. Hood Community College, Oregon

covered shelters where students can wait for bus or car pool; and safe convoy after dark to parking areas or bus stops.

Response to the University of Minnesota's express buses to the campus has been better than to its car pooling program. With approximately 40,000 commuting students, the university is the fourth largest traffic generator in the Twin Cities area.

Since 1970, the university and the Metropolitan Transit Commission (MTC) jointly have operated the University Express Bus System. Ten express bus routes come to the campus from different areas of Minneapolis, St. Paul, and the suburbs. The first buses arrive on campus about 7:30 A.M.

Additional buses arrive on the hour until about 10 A.M. Departures from campus begin about 2 P.M. with the largest number of people leaving about 3 or 4:30 P.M. The express buses are popular with faculty and civil service employees, as well as with students. Roger Huss, university transit coordinator, reports that in the fiscal year ending June, 1976, 462,000 persons rode the express buses, an increase of more than 150,000 from the previous year. There are more routes and more frequent trips on most of the routes. The express bus operation is not a moneymaking venture. The university and the MTC each pay half of the $120,000 deficit.

A computerized car pool, also organized by the university transit department, has been much less successful than the express bus operation. Of the 13,500 parking spaces on campus, 7,400 are available on a daily basis. Two lots are reserved until noon for car pool patrons and they are being used. There is free parking midway between the Minneapolis and St. Paul campuses, and persons using that lot may ride the bus at half fare. Write: *Ronaele Sayre, Information Representative, Department of University Relations, S-68 Morrill Hall, Minneapolis, Minn. 55455.*

The University of South Florida, predominantly a commuter institution, encourages students to use car pools through three systems:

☐ Ride boards on the first floor of the University Center and in some of the colleges help those seeking and offering rides to find each other.

☐ Zip Code Directories, another tool for identifying prospective riders, are located in each college dean's office. Car pools may coordinate class schedules and arrange travel hours by using the "free time" blocked out.

☐ TBART (Tampa Bay Area Rapid Transit Authority) continually surveys transportation patterns as a basis for mass transit development. Through the Student Government Office, TBART will furnish a computerized listing of prospective car pool members to students who request it. Write: *Charles F. Hewitt, Assistant to the Vice-President for Student Affairs, University of South Florida, Tampa, Fla. 33620.*

The University of Maryland's four 19-seat Mercedes buses do double duty, providing free bus service on three routes to campus in the morning and from campus in the afternoon, as well as responding to the Call-a-Ride service in off hours. Expansion is planned. Two of the regular routes run between local apartment complexes with high student populations and campus; the third is a "park and ride" arrangement using a local shopping center's parking lot. The vehicles arc also used for the evening shuttle bus service. Students may call a ride and get service to the parking lot or to a residence on or close to campus. The security police handle the evening calls. This service is particularly good for students who want to get from the library to the parking lot after midnight, especially freshmen whose parking lot is way out on the fringes of campus. Write: *Sylvia Stewart, Director, Office of Commuter Affairs, 1211 Student Union, University of Maryland, College Park, Md. 20742.*

Hood College, according to the Director of Continuing Education, is not going to spend a lot more on parking. The college is attacking its commuter transportation problem in other ways. As soon as students have their class schedules, the Dean of Continuing Education works up a car-pooling schedule that includes faculty and staff as well as students. The result is that a lot of communication and learning takes place during the ride. To increase the number of parking spaces, the college negotiated successfully with the town to change to diagonal parking on the street nearest the college. This has increased on-street parking by one third. Administrators believe that this can be done elsewhere not only in the vicinity of the campus but also in other college towns and cities. The continuing education department also favors charging resident students more for parking in order to cut down the cars on campus and leave more space for commuters, but as yet this has not been put into effect. Write: *Dixie Miller, Director, Department of Continuing Education, Hood College, Frederick, Md. 21701.*

Incentives to car-pooling have helped to cut down the number of parking spaces being used at Oakland University. Riders are matched up by computer, and ride pools are given preferred parking and a discount on the parking fee. Any time the number of ride pool spaces required exceeds those designated, the office of campus affairs adjusts the number and changes the reserve signs. Oakland, in a triangle about 50 miles or less from Detroit, Rochester, Pontiac, and their suburbs, has arranged also for public transportation links via buses to campus that are scheduled to coincide with student needs. A bus shelter has been erected on campus. Write: *Rosalind Andreas, Director of Commuter Services, Oakland University, Rochester, Mich. 48063.*

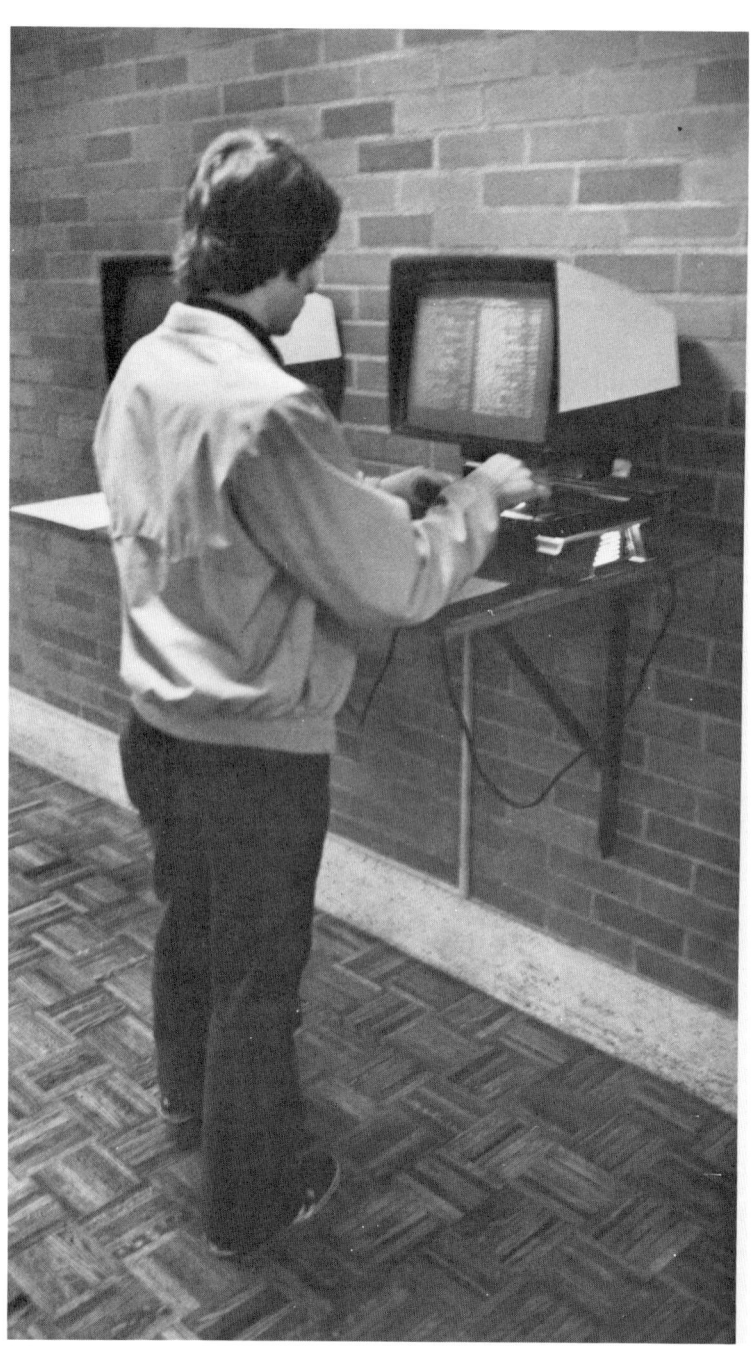

Erb Memorial Union, University of Oregon

Places To Get Information

The failure of commuting students to develop a strong identification with the college they are attending or to participate in scheduled activities is often due to the fact that they do not know what is going on. "Someone should devise a better mailbox," says Dr. Charles Hewitt, assistant to the vice-president for student affairs at the University of South Florida.

Residents have mailboxes, but the problem is how to communicate effectively with commuting students on a daily basis—South Florida has 23,000 commuters—and how to give them the positive identification with the campus that residents have. Few campuses, even with smaller commuter populations, have found space for a mailbox with each student's name and I.D. number on it or personnel to make daily deliveries, but many are attempting to bridge the communications gap in other ways.

The University of Minnesota-Minneapolis has message boards in the main library and in the departmental libraries where students can receive and leave messages for other students and for faculty. C.W. Post College and the University of Oregon's Erb Memorial Union both operate 24-hour "activity hot lines" so that students who are not on campus can telephone for information about upcoming events and make plans to attend.

Hood College's new dean of student affairs is working to get better scheduling of events, including a blank period during the day for group activities that will encourage communication between day and residential students.

The University of Massachusetts' Campus Assistance Center can be contacted for campus news 16 hours a day. The Associated Students of UCLA operates a telephone help line from 6 A.M. to 2 P.M. providing commuters with human support for personal or academic crises. At the University of Oregon closed circuit television monitors in the union restaurant, dormitory common areas, and some classrooms flash vital information, such as which classes are full and closed to registration, as well as providing local and national news.

"There is a dire need to get information to commuting students," says Steven Tibbitts, Director of Non-Residence Life at Kutztown State College. "They miss a lot of things because they don't hear about them in time. Commuting students simply do not have the time to do everything for themselves so we try to help them as much as possible." Two years ago Kutztown's Office of Non-Residence Life experimented with a "satellite office" consisting of a table in the snack bar in the student center, the hub of the commuters' nonclassroom life. On the table were places for flyers and messages; staff members were available two days a week to talk with students and answer questions. Signs were posted at strategic points to spread the word, and the student newspaper publicized the times at which members of the administration would be in the area. A survey of the 2,000 commuting students brought 600 responses, all favorable, and the satellite office was expanded. Hours are 9 A.M. to 3 P.M. in the lounge area. A commuter newsletter goes to the commuters' homes, with mailing costs paid by the student government. Write: *Steven Tibbitts, Director of Non-Residence Life, Kutztown State College, Kutztown, Pa. 19530.*

One way to stimulate commuting students to ask questions is to make the Office of Commuter Services highly visible. When Michigan's Oakland University decided to give more attention to commuters, the renovations on campus began with the modification of a prime location in the student center to house the office. Glass was used abundantly in partitions and dividers to give a "come on in" effect and make the service and the staff visible. Another tactic was to involve the students in planning the renovation and redecoration of spaces for their use. The office worked closely with the physical plant department on the modification of two classrooms into lounges. Students were responsible for choosing the decor, selecting colors of paint and furnishings, and ordering furniture through the Office of Student Affairs. The lounges are for the use of all students, so there is a good mix of residential and nonresidential users. The office hopes to get

Erb Memorial Union, University of Oregon

additional space for lounges in other classroom buildings, for many students their home on campus. Write: *Rosalind Andreas, Director of Commuter Services, Oakland University, Rochester, Mich. 48063.*

In the fall of 1976 the University of Maryland began using commuter assistants to give increased visibility to the needs of nonresidents and to help them keep in touch with campus life and activities. At first each assistant, working 15 hours a week, served as a generalist, responding to any request for help. In 1976-77, the roles are more specialized, with certain tasks assigned to each of the six commuter assistants. One is a commuter liaison with the town, attending town meetings and school board meetings, and communicating to townspeople and to students any information or actions affecting the interests of both. Another acts as liaison on campus to present the commuters' view to student organizations and to the administration. A commuter assistant edits the monthly newsletter which is mailed do the homes of commuting students. Another is transportation liaison, arranging for car pooling. A liaison resource person for programming calls the attention of faculty and staff to the time constraints and program needs of commuting students, so that the college can better satisfy them. Write: *Sylvia S. Stewart, Director, Commuter Student Affairs, 1195 Student Union Building, University of Maryland, College Park, Md. 20742.*

The primary problem perceived at Johns Hopkins was a lack of communication. Since commuting freshmen's mailboxes were separate from the main freshmen mailroom in the dorm, freshmen commuters often did not receive mail directed to the freshman class at large. To alleviate this problem, a number of sets of computer-prepared mailing labels were made up for special mailings to commuters.

Five students, selected by the Student Council to serve as a commuter committee, and some associate members prepared a commuter directory giving the names of all commuters. The committee also sent out a series of newsletters to keep commuters posted on upcoming events and special programs. The council also, after a survey of students, established a car-pool board and is trying to get times for social events that are acceptable to the majority of commuters. The committee also recommends greater publicity for the Athletic and Health Centers, about which commuters surveyed knew little. Write: *Dean of Students, Johns Hopkins University, Charles & 34th Streets, Baltimore, Md. 21218.*

The University of South Florida (USF) considers itself a prototype of the university of tomorrow, a metropolitan university with more than 90 percent of its more than 20,000 students commuting to campus daily. In 1973-74 USF decided to try reaching out to the commuting students by taking information to them in a place they could not miss—the commuter parking lots surrounding the campus. The first mobile Commuters Information Booth was a rented concession wagon that moved from lot to lot. Members of the student affairs staff and student leaders were on hand from 7:30 A.M.

to 6 P.M. to pass out information and answer questions. They had walkie-talkies for communicating with the Office of Student Affairs to get quick answers to tough questions.

The present Commuters Information Booth—a sort of glorified hotdog stand known as "Chuck's Wagon," named for the man who had the idea—was built by the physical plant department for approximately $600. Painted green and gold, the university colors, the booth serves as a contact point with commuters. A special effort is made to distribute information about programs aimed directly at commuting students such as matinees, commuter luncheons, crime prevention programs, car pooling, and booster or pep clubs to increase spectator support for intercollegiate athletics. Write: *Charles Hewitt, Assistant to the Vice-President for Student Affairs, University of South Florida, Tampa, Fla. 33620.*

Places To Leave Children

A recent phenomenon on college campuses is the child-care center where student-parents can leave their children while attending classes or college events. Often all that is needed to turn a classroom or other space into a satisfactory child-care facility are minor renovations, decorating, and simple furnishings. Sometimes the child-care center may serve a dual function, providing practical experience for college students interested in early childhood education, child psychology, or social work. Some centers specialize in short-term drop-in care while others take children by the day or week. Parents generally pay a modest fee, often according to their means, so that the center is at least partially self-supporting.

Many of Mount Mary College's students would not be able to attend classes if it were not for the child-care center, opened in 1973 in the basement of the main classroom building. The center, licensed by the State of Wisconsin as a short-term baby sitting service for students only, cares for about 20 children per hour. The charge is a minimal 60 cents per hour per child, and only 40 cents per hour for additional children of the same family. The college covers the balance of the cost for a professional director and student aides. The center contains two rooms, one of which is used for children from six months to three years old, the other for those over three years of age. Equipment is simple, consisting of small tables and chairs, toys, and games. There is no formal educational program but the director, a former teacher, points out that the children are learning all the time. Write: *Mrs. Halaska, Director, Child Care Center, Mount Mary College, Milwaukee, Wis. 53222.*

UCLA's Child Care Center was established through a cooperative effort of students, staff, faculty, and alumni concerned with the ongoing need of the campus community for day care. The governing board is made up of parents, faculty, and a chancellor's representative. The center, located in renovated space near the tennis courts and across from the Medical Center, cares for more than 100 children, some as young as two months. Parents pay on a sliding fee scale according to their means and volunteer time to assist the professional staff. A second facility for child care is housed in a university-owned home adjacent to the student union. It is operated by the Associated Students at Los Angeles California State University and offers two types of care—full day and hourly—for children of commuter students. Write: *Don Finley, Director, Associated Students of UCLA, Kerckhoff Hall, University of California, 405 Hilgard Avenue, Los Angeles, Calif. 90024.*

When a veterans co-op group leased an unfilled dormitory at Eastern Washington State College and filled it with 70 veterans and their families, the need for a day-care center became apparent. It operates on the ground floor of the veterans' dormitory but also serves college commuters as well. Write: *Director, Sutton Hall, Eastern Washington State College, Cheney, Wash. 99004.*

North Texas State University has two facilities for day care of children whose parents are students: Rivendell Pre-School, which specializes in all-day, weekly care, and the North Texas Day Care Center, specializing in morning or afternoon care while parents are in classes. Charges at Rivendell, which has a capacity of 27 children, are slightly less than at commercial day-care centers in the area. Rivendell opens at 7:15 A.M. during summer school to accommodate parents who have early morning classes. At the North Texas Day Care Center, children of commuters and those evidencing financial need are given preference. The regular rate is $2.00 per morning or afternoon session, $1.00 for those with financial need. The center operates on all class days. Children enrolled must have medical exams and be covered by personal insurance either by the parent or through the center. Write: *Dean of Students, North Texas State University, Denton, Tex. 76203.*

Places To Rest

Places to sleep—for a catnap or overnight—are in short supply on most campuses, even those with large commuting populations. From a study done by ACUHO (Association of College and University Housing Officers) it was determined that 41 percent of the institutions surveyed offer some form of temporary housing during the school year but only 14 percent offer such housing on other than an emergency basis. As the nonresidential student population grows and the residential segment shrinks—trends that are projected for the next few decades—facilities for rest and recreation for commuting students can no longer be considered frills. Institutions that have acted tentatively to provide a few bunks, beds, and showers in dormitory and lounge areas have been surprised by the student response. A few, such as Johns Hopkins University, have recognized the potential of overnight housing for integrating commuters into the campus life.

Mt. Hood Community College provides sleeping and shower facilities for commuting students, many of whom travel long distances, often have several hours between classes, and may come directly from work or go to work after class without a chance for a cleanup. The college encourages the students to use the hostel rather than lounges and cars for napping. The facility contains 12 bunk beds for women and 12 for men, with shower facilities for each. The bunks are equipped with vinyl-covered mattresses, and the college provides bedding, liquid soap, and large paper shower towels. An occupant may use his own bedroll instead of sleeping in a bunk. The only entrance to the sleeping quarters is through the male and female lounge and restroom areas. A low blue night light is conducive to sleep, yet allows for movement. There are regular work lights also. Groups participating in college activities may request overnight use of the hostel. The fee is $3.00, and a college staff member must stay overnight. Write: *Robert Jensen, Dean of Student Affairs, Mt. Hood Community College, 26000 S.E. Stark, Gresham, Ore. 97030.*

The University of Maryland will continue its study lodge again this year to provide sleeping space for commuters during exam week. Begun on an experimental basis in the fall of 1975, the lodge utilized a big open room in the dormitory community center to provide ten spaces for men and ten for women. Despite the lack of privacy, 39 men and 6 women used the lodge during the seven-day exam period. In the spring, it was decided to provide separate accommodations for men and women, utilizing space in the lounges of single-sex dormitories. During this exam period, 26 men and 10 women used the accommodations. Space is free to students but they have to preregister. Write: *Sylvia Stewart, Director, Office of Commuter Affairs, 1211 Student Union, University of Maryland, College Park, Md. 20742.*

Sarah Lawrence College keeps two rooms available in Mac-Cracken Hall for day students who want to spend the night on campus. Rooms must be reserved before 5 P.M. and may be used only two nights consecutively. There is a charge of $1.50 per night, plus a charge for linen if used. Write: *Cynthia Nosek, Director of Student Services, One Mead Way, Bronxville, N.Y. 10708.*

The University of Massachusetts' student center includes a hotel, where commuting students can stay overnight at a special rate. Music rooms in the center contain headphones and tape decks for music buffs who want temporary respite from their busy schedules. Free on-campus telephone service makes it easy for students to call other buildings to get information, check schedules, or talk to professors. Write: *Donald Witkoski, Accommodations Manager, University of Massachusetts, Campus Center, Amherst, Mass. 01003.*

Wesleyan University offers a gas-saver's option to graduate students enrolled in the summer session. The University holds back four double rooms at the start of the session, reserving them for people who live off-campus but find it desirable to stay overnight for a few nights per week. The housing office handles the rooms as if the facility were a motel, except that only a bed and room key are provided. The fee is $4.00 per night. The arrangement is popular with students who want to work in the library until midnight, for an actor whose rehearsal runs late, or for a visiting faculty member who is on campus only part of the week. Write: *Peter V. Buttenheim, Assistant Director, Graduate Summer School, Wesleyan University, Middletown, Ct. 06457.*

Administrators at Bronx Community College discovered that many students were living in situations not conducive to academic success, and that some were even sleeping on subways and park benches. As a result, one floor of a fraternity house that was not fully occupied was converted into eight rooms for transients. Students could stay in this emergency housing for one night to three weeks, at $3.00 per night, while the college helped them solve their housing problems. Unfortunately, when the city cut back its general funding for education, no special funds could be found for this project and it was terminated. Write: *Prof. Henrietta Whitcomb, College Discovery, CUNY, Bronx Community College, Lew Hall, 181st Street & University Avenue, Bronx, N.Y. 10453.*

Oklahoma State University has some rooms available on a demand basis in the hotel that is part of the student union. Students who are searching for apartments or who need an occasional get-away space, may register. A three-level parking garage adjoining the union also serves hotel residents and helps to ease the commuter parking crunch. Students and faculty staying overnight have access to the union's bowling alleys, game rooms, specialty shops, and a sweet shop which prepares pastries on site. Write: *Winston Schindell, Director of Student Union, Oklahoma State University, Stillwater, Okla. 74074.*

Commuter students at Iowa State University staged a demonstration to protest the inadequate facilities for commuters in the student union. As a result, a room was designated as a commuter lounge and showers and lockers were provided. Write: *Bruce Hudson, Director of the Student Union, Iowa State University, Ames, Iowa 50010.*

Johns Hopkins University is making an all-out effort to integrate commuter and dormitory students. One of its most successful programs is the commuter sleepover. During the summer, commuters and dorm residents are matched for compatibility and informed of their designated "dorm mate." During orientation week all commuters are invited to bring a sleeping bag and to stay with the residents with whom they are matched. During that week, they participate in dormitory social events and decisions. After considerable debate as to where the commuter lounge was to be located, a small lounge in the basement of the dormitory opened in the fall of 1976 for a trial run. Special education programs are being implemented to make commuters aware of the facilities that are generally underutilized by them, and parents of commuting students are given some orientation to remind them that their sons and daughters, although still living at home, now have different needs and activity patterns. Write: *Commuter Committee, Orientation Office, The Johns Hopkins University, Baltimore, Md. 21218.*

Although Kutztown State College has no sleeping facilities for commuting students, it does have showers and lockers, and the college is experimenting with ways to involve commuters in campus activities. In September 1976, scheduling returned to an earlier practice of having a free period during the day, from 11 A.M. to noon on Tuesday and Thursday, with no classes. This leaves the faculty free to hold office hours, which they are required to do five hours a week. Once a month there will be a major event during that hour, and once a month there will be no program or entertainment scheduled, so that the Office of Non-Residence Life can observe informally what students elect to do. "We'll try anything once, drop it if the response is not good," says Stephen Tibbitts, Director of Non-Residence Life. "Only about half the students indicated in advance that they want the free period but in practice the response may be different."

More than half of Kutztown State's commuters work more than 20 hours a week. They tend to be spectators at college events. A number of married students, in fact, wrote letters of appreciation when the student government arranged for spouses of married students to get ID cards for five dollars, allowing them to attend college events at student rates. Kutztown has noontime concerts but only minimal recreational facilities in the student center—a couple of ping pong tables, a pool table, and a snack bar—and the center closes at 4 P.M. There is not time between classes to show a two-hour movie, so students on campus at night go to the library or home. Tibbitts hopes that this will change as commuting students and college administrators come to understand each other better. Write: *Stephen Tibbitts, Director of Non-Residence Life, Kutztown State College, Kutztown, Pa. 19530.*

Places For Recreation

There is no reason to assume that the commuting student has less desire than his residential counterpart for fun and games. His participation in campus activities, however, is inevitably limited by transportation and time schedules, and his involvement—if there is to be any—must be encouraged by the right sorts of facilities and easy access to them. Commuters generally have to forego trying out for teams that have lengthy practice sessions late in the afternoon in favor of individual or small group activities that can begin and end at the participants' convenience. Their leisure comes in short segments, often at times when there are no scheduled events or the gymnasium and recreational areas are closed. They need opportunities for informal, unscheduled, casual entertainment than can be enjoyed in minutes instead of hours—places to bowl, swim, play cards, listen to music, operate the electronic games, or just to relax in an outdoor lounge or meeting place. Two-hour movies are seldom the answer, although the University of Wisconsin will experiment this year with afternoon movies to see if matinees draw commuting students.

The newer student unions—built or renovated in the 1970s after consultation with students—generally have provisions for unscheduled recreational activities, often providing equipment free or for a nominal rental fee. For example, the University of Oregon's addition to Erb Memorial Union provides space for billiards, table tennis, machine games, and shuffleboard. A sports club program operating from the union offers students a chance to participate in crew, bowling, soccer, skiing, judo, water polo, lacrosse, karate, sailing, rodeo, and rugby.

The old Dodge estate of 1,400 acres, the site of Oakland University, is in the process of being developed into a recreational and cultural area and the Office for Commuter Services is heavily involved. The area is known as "The Village." Many of the original barns and silos are still standing. A barn was renovated recently into a theater. The

Places for recreation

Ohio State University

University of California at Berkeley

Ohio State University

lower level is now being made into a multipurpose facility with a lounge, a place for partying, a place for students to "kick up" between classes, or to relax and enjoy the nonurban atmosphere. Bike paths and outdoor recreational areas are planned for Oakland students, more than 9,000 of whom are commuters. Write: *Rosalind Andreas, Director of Commuter Services, Oakland University, Rochester, Mich. 48063.*

Eastern Washington State University combines recreation with education, using its 30-foot high man-made rock mountain to teach mountaineering and to give students an opportunity to practice their mountain-climbing skills. The mountain, built at a cost of $28,000, offers a complete array of basic climbing problems that challenge the experienced climber as well as the beginner. Write: *Jon J. Danielson, Architectural Supervisor, Eastern Washington State University, Cheney, Wash. 99004.*

The Student Activities Building at the State University of New York in Morrisville, which opened in 1971, has become the center of college-community life. During the day, the building, which cost $2.7 million and contains 80,424 gross square feet, is used mainly as an academic center. In the evening, the same facilities are used for meetings, sports events, special entertainment, and informal recreation. Facilities include the following: gymnasium, theater, music room, swimming pool, snack bar, lounge, bowling alleys, and weight room. The bowling alleys are open five nights a week and weekends. Recreation tournaments are held in billiards, chess, bowling, and table tennis. The Fireplace Lounge is used for TV watching, for speakers, club parties, informal meetings, or just relaxing. The philosophy for combining academic, cultural, social, and recreational programs under one roof is that free-time activity is a learning experience in itself and that it influences study and education. The Student Activities Building, where students, faculty, and townspeople get to know each other, is seen as a positive force for overall personal development. Write: *George D. Homokay, Director of Student Activities, State University of New York Agricultural and Technical College, Morrisville, N.Y. 13408.*

Erb Memorial Union, University of Oregon

Places To Enjoy the Arts

Art, music, dance, and the theater offer very special opportunities for recreation and self-expression. They can be enjoyed independently or in a group, by spectators, by listeners, or by participants. For the majority of people, the arts are the means of cultural enrichment; for a few, they may lead to a career. For many, painting, singing, pottery making, leather work, and the pursuit of other arts and crafts as a hobby may provide a sense of accomplishment and a better understanding of the elements that go into a truly great work of art. These experiences, long accepted as part of a college education, will elude commuting students, however, unless institutions make an extraordinary effort to expose students to the arts. The ideal place in which to give the arts visibility is the busiest building on campus—the student union or activities center. The presence of art here and the evidence of facilities for the enjoyment of music, drama, dance, and a variety of crafts is bound to increase even a busy student's awareness, interest, and participation. Iowa State University's Memorial Union, for example, contains the university's permanent art collection, including a collection of miniature ships. There is piped-in music, and headphones are available for those desiring to listen to music of their own selection.

Oklahoma State's student union provides the setting for movies, dance, theater, art exhibits, and craft shows for those who want to participate as well as those who want to observe. The year-round film festival shows both American and European films. Performances of ballet, modern, and folk dance groups are regularly scheduled in the meeting rooms. A theater with thrust stage is used by both campus theater groups and professional performers; its foyer is used as an art gallery. The Georgian lounge doubles as a gallery for changing art exhibitions. And for students interested in crafts, Granny's Trunk specializes in the sale of pottery and other handcrafted products. Write: *Winston Shindell, Director, Student Union, Oklahoma State University, Stillwater, Okla. 74074.*

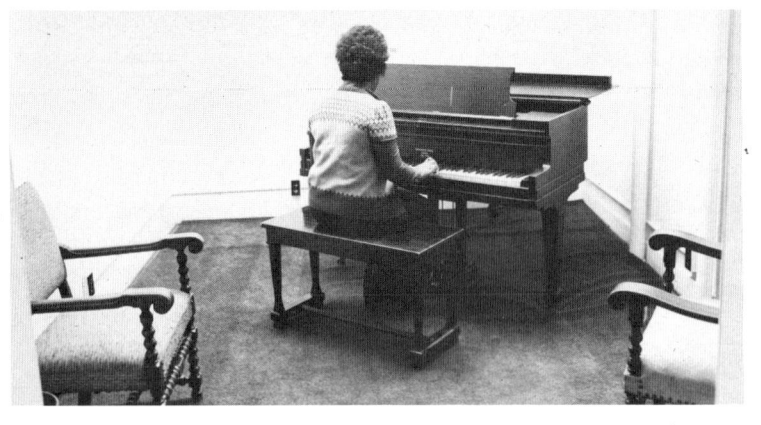

University of Oregon students unable to enroll in regular art classes, which are often oversubscribed, may now use the craft center at the enlarged Erb Memorial Union. A professional staff offers introductory courses for those wanting formal instruction. For a nominal fee, participants may work with ceramics, fabric, leather, graphics, jewelry, photography, and wood. Products of the craft shop, particularly the ceramic pots for plants, are on display throughout the union. A graphic artist is available to help individuals and groups with silk screening and other poster techniques. The Cultural Forum, operating out of the union, brings to the campus a wide variety of exhibitions and persons involved in the arts, including authors, poets, and performing artists. Write: *Adell McMillan, Director of the Student Union, Erb Memorial Union, University of Oregon, Eugene, Ore. 97403.*

California State University in Los Angeles offers a variety of opportunities for cultural enrichment. Galleries on the first floor of the student union exhibit the university's permanent art collection as well as changing exhibits. A music browsing area provides listening rooms where students may listen to the piped-in music they select while they study, relax, or nap. In the craft center, students can work in whatever medium they wish at their own convenience. Oversized landings and corridors surrounding a five-story enclosed court were designed especially for public theater performances. An outdoor amphitheater adjacent to the union was also designed to accommodate the performing arts. Write: *Roger Godesen, Director of the Student Union, California State University, 5151 State University Drive, Los Angeles, Calif. 90032.*

Exhibition space for faculty and student art works is credited with generating interest in the arts at California Polytechnic State University at San Luis Obispo. Evening art courses held at the craft center in the new Julian A. McPhee University Union are reported to be overenrolled constantly. The center is also open for informal work during the day. Exhibition space is provided for sculpture, ceramics, and photography by faculty members and students, as well as for traveling exhibitions. The union's auditorium has adequate stage and lighting equipment for use by student theater groups and visiting professionals. Write: *Dennis Ruthenbeck, Building Manager of Associated Student Union, California Polytechnic State University, San Luis Obispo, Calif. 93407.*

Commuting students at Northwestern University in Evanston can use their waiting or down time pleasantly and productively in the Music Listening and Browsing Library. They may choose a stereo or quadraphonic room furnished with carpeted mounds for reclining and listening. Individuals or groups may elect to listen to classical or modern electronic music from the library's collection, or they may take their own. The library also contains periodicals, reference books, and specialty publications in the fields of music and the visual arts. Informal exhibits of student art works as well as traveling shows are displayed in the area. Write: *John Duffek, Director of Norris University Center, Northwestern University, 1999 Sheridan Road, Evanston, Ill. 60201.*

Students at SUNY's Morrisville campus can no longer complain that there are no cultural events and nothing to do on campus. The completion of the Student Activities Building in 1971 changed all that, bringing to campus a variety of activities never previously available in this rural community. Drama classes held in the 400-seat theater attract about 60 students per year, while 150 students per year take music and art in the studio. Individual art tutoring is available. The building also serves as a community center, bringing together students and townspeople for many events. Morrisville President N. Royson Whipple ranks the Student Activities Building as the most versatile and most valuable building on campus. "Full utilization will come," he says, "not only for planned uses but also for a multitude of activities that were not even dreamed of by the planners." Write: *George D. Homokay, Director of Student Activities, State University of New York Agricultural and Technical College, Morrisville, N.Y. 13408.*

Oakland University, 90 percent of whose students are commuters, still manages to achieve a high level of student involvement in campus activities. Student Enterprises operates both a film society and a theater. Theater productions are staged in the Barn Theatre, first of the farm structures to be renovated in The Village, an area of campus containing a number of farm buildings that members of the university community plan to renovate into cinema and concert halls and facilities for a multiplicity of cultural, education, and social activities. The Student Enterprise Theatre began operation in 1962. It offers four productions a year that are open to students, faculty, and staff for performing opportunities as well as technical work. Traditionally, the Barn Theatre offers a balanced season that includes a musical, a drama, a comedy, and a dance production. The Student Enterprise Film Society is an outgrowth of random film showings on and off campus. The society now has a regular weekly series with showings on Tuesday, Friday, Saturday, and Sunday evenings. Films vary from art classic to modern experimental films and current-run popular movies. The society also has equipment for the production of new films by student film makers. Write: *Rosalind Andreas, Director of Commuter Services, Oakland University, Rochester, Mich. 48063.*

Places To Shop

Shopping—either for necessaries or on impulse—is an activity for which commuting students have little time. To sell to them, one has to catch them on the run. Shops that are a convenience for students, however, can be a source of income for the college or university and for the student associations that often manage the small businesses on campus.

Two of the most popular shops at the University of Milwaukee's Greene Commons are the plant shop and the general store. The Plant Convention not only offers plants for sale but also holds classes in which students can learn the basics of plant care such as potting, watering, and feeding. The old-fashioned country store, known as The Emporium, has cookies, pastries, and cakes baked on the premises. The store's delicatessen has a variety of meats, cheeses, and salads, and serves a soup-and-sandwich luncheon special Monday through Friday. Shelves are stocked with soft drinks, tobacco products, magazines, school supplies, prepackaged grocery items, and sundries. Write: *Elmer E. Hamann, Director of Housing, The University of Wisconsin, Milwaukee, Wis. 53201.*

UCLA's bookstore claims to be the largest campus bookstore in the United States. Enlarged recently to 24,000 square feet, the store does not restrict its stock to books. Besides academic and trade books, the store handles art and engineering supplies, cosmetics, electronic calculators, stereos, radios, and dozens of personal and household items with UCLA imprinted on them. There is an extensive sportswear department. The store also offers services, including lecture note and xerox services, book information, and a buy-back book service. Some services duplicate what is offered in other parts of the union, but convenience is the key. Write: *Don Finley, Director, Associated Students of UCLA, Kerckhoff Hall, University of California, 405 Hilgard Avenue, Los Angeles, Calif. 90024.*

Oklahoma State University's student union offers commercial space to private leasing agents, thus generating income for the university and enabling the union to offer commodities that would not be available otherwise. Among the shops are a travel agency, men's and women's clothing stores, boutiques, jewelry, gift, candy, and hobby shops, a flower mart, and men's and women's barbershops. Write: *Winston Schindell, Director of Student Union, Oklahoma State University, Stillwater, Okla. 74074.*

The buildings around Berkeley's Sproul Plaza, including the student center completed about ten years ago, have stood up well, adequately serving the purposes for which their designers and the University of California intended them. One main facility in the center, however, has been totally redesigned. The original student store, which followed a discount-store layout with checkout counters like a large supermarket, was a financial failure. It was torn out during 1968-69 and reconstructed to follow the interior street concept originally advocated by the architect. An enclosed pedestrian street is lined with what seem to be individual stores; in reality they form the spine of a department store under central management but without layered departments. Access to the stores is from the interior street only, but it can be entered from three separate points on the lower plaza. The management of the shops is a tenant of the university, paying rent to the Berkeley Student

Association. The association, in turn, is responsible for maintaining and servicing the facility. The enclosed pedestrian street of shops generates its own traffic. Write: *Gerald Brown, Executive Director, Associated Students, University of California, 207 Eshleman Hall, Berkeley, Calif. 94720.*

The University of Wisconsin's bookstore on the Milwaukee campus occupies 25,000 square feet on two levels in the union and grosses $2 million annually. Revenue comes from the usual range of goods—books, cards, candles, supplies, clothes, gifts, periodicals, candy, tobacco, and sundries—and from a number of special services, such as typewriter rentals. Sheet music for guitar and piano was added recently. Because stores are commercial ventures, their response to student demand and preference is direct and swift. UWM's bookstore manager keeps a suggestion box near the front of the store and frequently changes store policy and operations in line with student comments. The textbook department remains self-service, despite some shoplifting, because students desire to look at books for other courses than those for which they are registered in order to plan ahead for the next semester. Last fall, the store was calling attention to the newly designed shopping bags that are biodegradable and will not release noxious gases if burned. Write: *Doug Arthur, Manager, UWM Book Store, Milwaukee, Wis. 53201.*

Other Services

The basic needs of commuting students are the same as the daily needs of people everywhere regarding places to mail letters, cash checks, copy papers, rent equipment, get information, and receive counseling and legal aid. Although these needs are not exclusive to commuters, their situation is special in that what little free time they have often occurs when they are on campus. Colleges and universities are beginning to respond positively with some of the extras.

Orientation and Counseling

Johns Hopkins University's program to integrate commuters into the campus life is entirely student-run under the auspices of the Office of Residential Life. The program is about three years old and is being expanded and refined each year. A major facet of the commuter orientation program is counseling. A group of about 20 upperclassmen commuters are designated as commuter counselors. They meet with small groups of incoming freshmen commuters during the summer preceding entrance, advise them on life at Hopkins and try to give them a head start. With out-of-town students, the commuting student is cast in the role of host. Commuters help dorm resident freshmen move into their rooms and take them on tours of the commuters' native Baltimore or serve food at one of the first-week receptions, all practical ways for commuters and residents to get acquainted. As an offshoot of the commuter program, a series of special social programs has come into existence. All feature life in Baltimore and the surrounding communities. A "Back to Baltimore" party on the first weekend after winter vacation welcomes the returning out-of-town students. Throughout the year, commuters are encouraged to show residents around the city and to accompany them to ethnic restaurants and community events.

Stephen Tibbitts, Director of Non-Residence Life at Kutztown State College, points out that, while the average age of commuters may be higher than residential students, there are still large numbers of 17- and 18-year-olds who need the same sort of counseling that resident assistants in the dorms furnish. Kutztown now has six upperclass commuter advisors on duty in a satellite office in the student center to reach commuting students and help them with any problems they may have. This fall for the first time an amateur videotape will be shown during orientation, showing the Office for Commuter Services (Non-Residential), the satellite office in the student center with the student advisor's table, and publicizing the availability of faculty and administration. The message: Come to us for anything, any sort of information. If we don't have it, we'll get it for you.

At the University of Maryland, each commuter assistant is expected to develop peer counseling relationships and a supportive group association with 25 or more persons. Assistants are responsible for providing information for commuters about financial aid, career development, academic advisement, and health services; for sponsoring study sessions and tutorial groups; for aiding with housing problems off-campus, and for establishing research teams to explore and suggest ways to improve basic services to commuters such as food, transportation, academic advisement, recreation, and library services.

Information
A Dial Access information program for students was inaugurated last year by the University of Minnesota's Campus Assistance Center. Students may call from 8 A.M. to 8 P.M. weekdays and from noon to 5 P.M. on the weekends and request a specific tape on any one of a number of subjects, such as how to register, how to get an advisor, and birth control and venereal disease information. The university plans to initiate a legal services program for all fee-paying students next spring.

Check Cashing
Branch banks like the one in C.W. Post College's Hillwood Commons are showing up on a number of campuses. The Associated Students at UCLA offers a check-cashing service for postdated checks. For a 35-cent fee, the check will be held

two weeks before being sent to the bank for clearance. This service has been in operation for over a year and has cashed checks for $2 million, some of which has been reinvested in sales and services at the union.

Typewriters and Business Machines

The bookstore at the University of Wisconsin-Milwaukee introduced a typewriter rental service last year. Electric typewriters are available weekly or monthly, with the fee payable in advance.

The University of South Florida has key punch machines and calculators for student use in the College of Business Administration and in the Science Center. The Social and Behavioral Sciences has a room with calculators, and both the business department and the library have rooms with typewriters for students. There are 19 machines in the library.

The Department for Student Organizations at Oakland University maintains a low-cost copy service and a student work area that includes mimeo and duplicating machines, typewriters, and counter space. Recycled paper is available at no cost.

The print shop in Erb Memorial Union at the University of Oregon provides offset printing, copying, binding, collating, and sign-making services at reasonable prices to students, faculty, and staff.

Equipment Rental

At Kutztown State College, administrators and students took a look at the student activities fund to see how some of it could be used so that commuting students would benefit. The result: a "free" rental service where students who live off-campus can borrow a vacuum cleaner, an ironing board (to be shared by four or five users living together or near each other), rug shampooers, and jumper cables—a popular item that allows students to get their cars started without calling an expensive tow truck. Oakland University also reports that jumper cables and tool kits are the rental items most in demand.

High interest in outdoor recreation at the University of Oregon provided the impetus for the Erb Memorial Union to organize extensive rental service of sports equipment and to offer instruction in its use. An outdoor resource center sells or rents skis, boots, poles, camping equipment, and other items. The canoe shack rents canoes and kayaks complete with car carriers. For a fee, students may attend workshops on camping, rock climbing, kayaking, and sailing. For indoors, a resale center carries bowling and billiard equipment.

Lockers

Places for commuters to hang their hats are in short supply on every campus surveyed. The Office of Commuter Services at Oakland University has succeeded in getting some lockers in classrooms and is pushing for more both in existing buildings and in ones under construction. Lockers to hold music have been added in the music building, and lockers for lab coats are being installed in the science building, so that commuters will not be loaded down with baggage. The office has also worked closely with the designer of the new classroom and office building now going up on the campus to make sure that an adequate number of lockers—and some vending machines—will be provided.

Managing the Change

Commuting students obviously are gaining advocates slowly. Once college and university administrators have adjusted their perceptions of commuting students and have acknowledged their numbers and needs, managing for the future may not prove to be as difficult as feared.

Any fears that administrators may have that adapting to commuting students will cause major upheavals in organization and costs seem to be unfounded. What appears to be needed is a shift in the way of looking at student services, and a greater flexibility about where, how, and when the services will be provided. The cry of commuting students is that institutions have no understanding or concern for the great diversity of life-styles and time schedules in most student bodies.

Costs reported by institutions that are trying to serve their commuting populations better are minimal. Capital outlays are frequently covered by franchise and leasing arrangement. Reallocating or converting underused space for new functions seldom requires a major capital expenditure. Student unions would have had to be replaced or modernized if all students were residents—and more dormitories would be required.

Many operating costs, instead of being added to budgets, are compensated in part by revenue generated from franchised food services, vending machines, coin-operated lockers, copying services, and other self-generating enterprises. Student organizations—once commuting students have made enough of an inroad to be heard—often handle sports equipment rentals, car pooling, food services, and store management.

Only one change to campus organization charts is directly attributable to commuters. This is the addition of a director and an office of commuter services. On most campuses, the functions are still handled within the office of student affairs, often by an assistant director with responsibility for commuter affairs. This gives less visibility to commuter concerns than a separate office, but it may have the converse advantage of closer integration of commuters into the total student body. In any case, the functions being performed by the rare office of commuter services or its more common equivalent give some valuable insight into what is involved in effective planning and management for commuting students.

The role of the director of commuter services, as seen by those who hold the title, is as follows:

☐ To be an advocate. The greatest need of commuting students, say those who work with them directly, is for an advocate who will publicize their concerns and get them a fair hearing. The primary responsibility of the office for commuter services is to publicize the needs of its constituents and to win understanding for their requests.

One way that is being used to achieve this is to make sure that commuting students are represented in every student organization, particularly in student government, and on all campus committees. Another technique for strengthening the commuter students' voice is to establish a student commuter council, as Oakland University has done, to hear commuter problems and to represent commuter interests.

☐ To coordinate with other departments. Planning and management that will be to the advantage of commuting students involve working with every department on campus, not just student affairs. Finding solutions to commuter problems must be done jointly with the persons responsible for physical facilities, transportation, food services, the library, the business office, and sometimes even dormitory personnel. Changes in scheduling can involve faculty or the manager of the student union. The Amherst Campus Center at the University of Massachusetts is now open from 7 A.M. to 2 P.M., and one restaurant stays open around the clock. The unions at C.W. Post in New York and Oklahoma State University have information desks that are open at all times. When renovations or new buildings are under consideration—or when any sort of long-range plans are being made—it is obligatory for commuting students to be represented in discussions with campus planners and architects.

☐ To act as a political influence. Getting commuters on all campus boards and organizations so that they will have input is only one aspect of the political role. There is also a need to build a bridge between commuting students and the administration, between the residents of the town or city in which the college is located; and between local government officials, such as the department of transportation and the highway department. In the case of publicly funded institutions, this influence must extend to the state legislature whose support for buildings and programs is essential.

☐ To research and evaluate needs and how they are being met. Keeping an up-to-date profile of students and their life-styles, through surveys and studies of facilities use and behavior patterns outside of class, is vital if services are to remain current with the trends in the student population. Directors of commuter students report that they frequently participate in studies with the office of institutional research and work with other professionals, such as members of the sociology department, on interpretations of the data.

Although these objectives simply extend what college management has always done—but with an eye on the special interests of commuters—some institutions have decided that it may be more efficient and economical to delegate responsibility for commuter affairs to a separate department. Oakland University in Rochester, Michigan, is a typical example of this approach.

Oakland's Office of Commuter Services opened in 1971. Its annual operating budget is $38,000. This includes the salaries of a director; a secretary; and a staff of 12 students, whose part-time work is about the equivalent of three or four full-time personnel; and supplies and services, including computer service. The staff is assisted by a student intern from the student activities office.

About 90 percent of Oakland's 10,500 students now commute. Beyond budgetary concerns and responsibility to commuting students, the activities of the Office of Commuter Services are determined by the special needs of subgroups within the commuter population—older students, women, minorities, the handicapped—and by the need to insure adequate facilities for commuters in future buildings. Most handicapped, for example, are commuters. The University of Oregon took this into account when it designed and built the addition to Erb Memorial Union, making it totally barrier free. San Francisco State University, on the other hand, neglected to do this, putting its student lounges in twin towers that were inaccessible to disabled students. The U.S. Department of Housing and Urban Development has decreed that the oversight must be corrected, making the towers accessible to everyone.

The challenge to administrators in serving commuter students is twofold: to raise their own and their colleagues' consciousness and commitment to their new clientele, and to strive for practical outcomes that will serve that clientele's needs.

National Clearinghouse for Commuter Programs

The primary focus of the National Clearinghouse for Commuter Programs is on students in higher education who do not live in residence halls. The clearinghouse was designed to collect and disseminate information about new, old, successful, unsuccessful, established, and experimental' programs affecting commuter students. It exists to facilitate the exchange and sharing of data concerning characteristics, attitudes, needs, and behaviors of commuter students among schools interested and/or involved in programs related to the student living off campus.

The University of Maryland Commuter Affairs Office currently serves as coordinator of the National Clearinghouse for Commuter Programs. The clearinghouse provides subscribers with synopses of current research, descriptions of projects underway, and opportunities to exchange ideas and request suggestions in a newsletter, *The Commuter.*

Membership is $20.00 per year. Make checks payable to The University of Maryland and send to the National Clearinghouse for Commuter Programs, Student Union, Room 1195, University of Maryland, College Park, Md. 20742.

EFL Publications

The following publications are available from EFL,
850 Third Avenue, New York, N.Y. 10022.
Prices include postage if orders are prepaid.

ARTS AND THE HANDICAPPED: AN ISSUE OF ACCESS Over 150 examples of how arts programs and facilities have been made accessible to the handicapped, from tactile museums to halls for performing arts, and for all types of handicaps. Emphasis on the laws affecting the handicapped. (1975) $4.00

THE ARTS IN FOUND PLACES Where and how the arts are finding homes in recycled buildings, and in the process often upgrading urban centers and neighborhoods. (1976) $7.00

CAMPUS IN TRANSITION Interprets demographic factors influencing college enrollments, discusses current academic trends, and describes how colleges are producing new income and/or providing new programs without building new facilities. (1975) $4.00

CAREER EDUCATION FACILITIES Programming guide for shared facilities making one set of spaces or equipment serve several purposes. (1973) $2.00

COMMUNICATIONS TECHNOLOGY IN HIGHER EDUCATION—REVISITED Twenty-one profiles that were distributed during 1975–76 in *Planning for Higher Education* update most of what has happened in this field during the last decade. 11x8½ reprints for $7.00 from Communications Press, Inc., 1346 Connecticut Avenue, N.W., Washington, D.C. 20036. Hardbound and paperbound editions available in Summer, 1977 from CPI.

COMMUNITY/SCHOOL: SHARING THE SPACE AND THE ACTION How schools share facilities with other public agencies to provide improved social services. The book discusses financing, planning, building, staffing, and operating community/schools. (1973) $4.00

FEWER PUPILS/SURPLUS SPACE Looks at the phenomenon of shrinking enrollments, its extent, its possible duration, and some of the strategies being developed to cope with unused school space. (1974) $4.00

FIVE OPEN PLAN HIGH SCHOOLS Text, plans, and pictures explain how secondary schools operate open curriculums in open spaces. (1973) $3.00

FOUR FABRIC STRUCTURES Tent-like or air-supported fabric roofs provide large, column-free spaces for physical recreation and student activities at less cost than conventional buildings. (1975) $3.00

GENERATING REVENUE FROM COLLEGE FACILITIES Strategies used by institutions of higher education to produce income from their land and buildings. (1974) Single copies free, multiple copies 50 cents each.

THE GREENING OF THE HIGH SCHOOL How to make secondary school healthy. Includes open curriculums and alternative education programs. (1973) $2.00

HIGH SCHOOL: THE PROCESS AND THE PLACE Planning, design, environmental management, and the behavioral and social influences of school space. (1972) $3.00

HOUSING FOR NEW TYPES OF STUDENTS Colleges faced with declining enrollments from the traditional age-group should widen their constituency by modifying their accommodations for senior citizens, those over 25, those under 18, the handicapped, married, single parents, etc. (1977) $4.00

MEMO TO AMBULATORY HEALTH CARE PLANNERS A general guide to making health centers more humane and flexible. (1976) $2.00

THE NEGLECTED MAJORITY: FACILITIES FOR COMMUTING STUDENTS Advocates making college facilities more amenable and available to students who do not live on campus. Includes examples of facilities for studying, eating, leisure, shopping, resting, recreation, etc. (1977) $4.00

NEW PLACES FOR THE ARTS Describes 49 museums, performing arts facilities, and multi-use centers. Includes listings of the consultants. (1976) $5.00

PATTERNS FOR DESIGNING CHILDREN'S CENTERS For people planning to operate children's centers. (1971) $3.95

PHYSICAL RECREATION FACILITIES Places providing good facilities for physical recreation in schools and colleges—air shelters, roofing existing stadiums, shared facilities, and conversions. (1973) $3.00

THE PLACE OF THE ARTS IN NEW TOWNS Approaches for developing arts programs and facilities in new towns and established communities. Insights and models for the support of the arts, the use of existing space, and financing. (1973) $3.00

REUSING RAILROAD STATIONS Advocates the reuse of abandoned stations for combined public and commercial purposes, including arts and educational centers, transportation hubs, and focal points for downtown renewal. (1974) $4.00

REUSING RAILROAD STATIONS BOOK TWO Furthers the advocacy position of the first book and explains the intricacies of financing the development of a railroad station. (1975) $4.00

THE SECONDARY SCHOOL: REDUCTION, RENEWAL, AND REAL ESTATE Warns of the forthcoming decline in high school enrollments. Suggestions for reorganizing schools to prevent them from becoming empty and unproductive. (1976) $4.00

SPACE COSTING: WHO SHOULD PAY FOR THE USE OF COLLEGE SPACE? Describes a technique for cost accounting the spaces and operating and maintenance expenses to the individual units or programs or an institution. (1977) $4.00

SURPLUS SCHOOL SPACE: OPTIONS & OPPORTUNITIES Tells how districts have averted closed schools by widening educational and social services, increasing career and special education programs. Advises how to make local enrollment projections, and how to decide whether to close or not. (1976) $4.00

STUDENT HOUSING A guide to economical ways to provide better housing for students. Illustrates techniques for improvement through administrative changes, remodeling old dorms, new management methods, co-ops, and government financing. (1972) $2.00

TECHNICAL ASSISTANCE FOR ARTS FACILITIES: A SOURCEBOOK Where arts groups can find help to establish their own studios, auditoriums, etc. Lists federal, state, and private sources. (1977) Free

WE'RE PLEASED THAT YOU ARE INTERESTED IN MAKING THE ARTS ACCESSIBLE TO EVERYONE... Describes arts programs and facilities that have been designed to overcome barriers to children, the elderly, and the handicapped. Contains an enrollment card for a free information service. (1976) Free

SCHOOLHOUSE A newsletter on financing, planning, designing, and renovating school facilities. Free

Films

The following films are available for rental at $9.00, or for purchase at $180.00 from New York University Film Library, 26 Washington Place, New York, N.Y. 10003. Telephone (212) 598-2250.

NEW LEASE ON LEARNING
A 22-minute, 16mm color film about the conversion of "found space" into a learning environment for young children. The space, formerly a synagogue, is now the Brooklyn Block School, one of New York City's few public schools for children aged 3–5.

ROOM TO LEARN
A 22-minute, 16mm color film about The Early Learning Center in Stamford, Connecticut, an open-plan early childhood school with facilities and program reflecting some of the better thinking in this field.

THE CITY: AN ENVIRONMENTAL CLASSROOM
A 28-minute, 16mm color film, produced by EFL in cooperation with the New York City Board of Education, shows facilities and resources in and around the city in which effective programs of environmental education are under way. Such diverse sites as the Hudson River, an incinerator, Chinatown, Governors Island, and a children's camp in a rural setting are analyzed for their contributions to the education of city children.

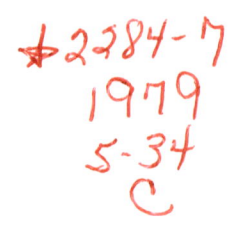